YOUNG MARTIN'S PROMISE

by Walter Dean Myers

Alex Haley, General Editor

Illustrations by
Barbara Higgins Bond

RSVP
RAINTREE
STECK-VAUGHN
PUBLISHERS
The Steck-Vaughn Company

Austin, Texas

Published by Steck-Vaughn Company.

Text, illustrations, and cover art copyright © 1993 by Dialogue Systems, Inc., 627 Broadway, New York, New York 10012. All rights reserved.

Cover art by Barbara Higgins Bond

Printed in the United States of America   9 10 11 12 - VH - 03 02 01

Library of Congress Cataloging-in-Publication Data

Myers, Walter Dean, 1937–
    Young Martin's promise / Walter Dean Myers; illustrator, Barbara Higgins Bond.
        p. cm.—(Stories of America)
    Summary: Relates events in Martin Luther King, Jr.'s, childhood which sowed the seeds for his activism for equal rights for people, regardless of their color.
    ISBN 0-8114-7210-8.—ISBN 0-8114-8050-X (pbk.)
    1. King, Martin Luther, Jr., 1929–1968—Childhood and youth—Juvenile litera-ture. 2. Afro-Americans—Biography—Juvenile literature. 3. Baptists—United States—Clergy—Biography—Juvenile literature. 4. Civil rights workers—United States—Biography—Juvenile literature. 5. Afro-Americans—Civil rights—Juvenile literature. 6. Afro-Americans—Segregation—Juvenile literature. [1. King, Martin Luther, Jr., 1929–1968—Childhood and youth. 2. Civil rights workers. 3. Afro-Americans—Biography.] I. Bond, Barbara Higgins, ill. II. Title. III. Series.
E185.97.K5M94 1993
323'.092—dc20
[B]   •   92–18070
                                                                              CIP
                                                                               AC

ISBN 0-8114-7210-8 (Hardcover)
ISBN 0-8114-8050-X (Softcover)

A Note
from Alex Haley, General Editor

Sticks and stones may break my bones, but words can never harm me. You've heard that one before, haven't you? If you have, you know it's only half true. Sticks and stones *may* break your bones. Words, though, can and do harm you, too.

Rules are made up of words. Rules can do a lot of harm if they're unfair. They can even take away your freedom. And there isn't a greater harm than that in the world.

This is a story about a young boy who felt the pain of unfair rules. It is a story about how he learned that you can change what is wrong.

Martin Luther King, Jr., grew up in Atlanta, Georgia, in the 1930s. When he was a little boy, Martin liked to climb trees. He also liked to play tag or catch with his friends on Auburn Avenue.

Two of his best friends lived across the street from him. Like Martin, they were good ballplayers and they were fast too. But most of all, they were good friends.

4

5

6

Things began to change when Martin and his friends started school. Martin hoped that he and his friends would go to school together. But in 1935 there were places where black children could not go to the same school as white children.

When the bus came to pick up Martin on the first day of school, his friends were not on it. All the children on the bus were black. All the children at Martin's school were, too.

When Martin got home from school that day, he was very excited. He couldn't wait to tell his friends about his first day of school. As he jumped off the school bus, he saw that some of his friends were already playing ball.

8

Martin ran over to them. He wanted to join the game, as he always did. But this time the other children stopped playing.

Our parents say we can't play with you anymore, his friend told Martin.

Martin asked why not.

His friends said that it was because they were white and Martin was black.

That's why we don't go to the same school, another boy told Martin. Martin had to go to the black school.

Martin did not know what to say. He swallowed hard and went back across the street slowly. He was very upset. Martin knew he had not done anything wrong. At dinner that night, he told his parents what had happened.

Martin's mother felt sorry for her son. In a calm voice, she told him about segregation. Segregation means keeping things or people apart. The law said that black people and white people could not be together in some places, such as school.

Segregation was not Martin's fault, but it still made him feel bad. He did not know why things had to be that way. Why couldn't kids just be friends?

14

Martin tried to forget what had happened. He made new friends at school. He still played ball and tag. But other things happened to remind him of how things were.

One day Martin's father was going for a drive downtown. Martin went with him. He liked to go downtown to see all of the shops and busy people. Since Martin needed new shoes, they decided to stop at a shoe store.

Martin ran over to the shoe store where he saw a pair he liked. They went inside and sat in the first empty seats they saw. The seats were near the front window, and Martin could see the shoes he wanted. A young clerk came up to them.

"I'll be happy to wait on you if you'll just move to those seats in the rear," the clerk said in a low voice.

"There's nothing wrong with these seats," Martin's father said. "We are quite comfortable here."

"Sorry," said the clerk, "but you will have to move to the rear of the store."

"We'll either buy shoes sitting here," Martin's father said, "or we won't buy shoes at all."

"Stop being so high and mighty!" the clerk said angrily. "That is the only place we serve black people."

Martin looked up at his father. Why was the man yelling at them? Why was he angry? All they wanted to do was to buy a pair of shoes.

Then Martin's father took his hand, and they walked out of the store—without buying the shoes.

As they drove back home, Martin saw
that his father was angry, too. He asked
his father what had happened. Why was
the clerk mad if they hadn't done
anything wrong?

It was part of segregation, Martin's
father explained. Making black people go
to the back of the store was not a law. It
was a custom. Customs are the ways in

which people expect to live. Many white people did not expect to sit with black people when they shopped. The clerk was mad because Martin's father would not go to the back.

"Segregation is stupid and cruel," Martin's father said. "I'll always fight against it."

24

Tears came to Martin's eyes. He hated it when people treated other people so meanly.

"I'll help you fight against segregation," Martin said, looking up at his father. "I'll help all I can."

From that day on, Martin tried to keep the promise he had made. He never forgot his friends or what happened in the shoe store. He thought about the pain he and his father had felt. He even thought about how upset the clerk had been. He knew that anything that made people feel that bad was wrong.

Back on Auburn Avenue, Martin often saw the boys who had been his friends. They still played ball, but without Martin. He would still speak to them in a friendly manner when he saw them. If their ball rolled across the street, he would still throw it back to them. Maybe they had to accept segregation, he thought, but he didn't.

When Martin Luther King, Jr., became a man, he worked hard to end segregation. He asked lawmakers to change the laws that kept people apart. He led people as they marched to protest the unfair treatment of black people. He spoke to thousands of people. He said that bringing people together was better than keeping them apart. He told them of his dream that all children would one day play and study together.

Because of Martin Luther King, Jr., and others like him, the segregation laws were changed. So were the customs that keep people apart. Now all children can go to the same schools. Because of Martin Luther King, Jr., kids of all colors can just be friends.

31

Martin Luther King Day

Martin Luther King Day is our youngest national holiday. It was created in 1983 and is celebrated on the third Monday in January. We celebrate this day because Martin Luther King was a great American hero.

Throughout his life Dr. King helped many people. He did not believe in fighting or hurting other people. He spoke about peace and brotherhood. He taught others to be peaceful, too.

Martin Luther King helped bring many great changes to this country. He dreamed of a world where everyone lived together in peace. He dreamed of a world where everyone is treated fairly and with respect. A good way to celebrate Martin Luther King Day is to make Martin Luther King's dream your dream.